MW01595015

Threescore & Ten... WOW!

Agnes Durant Pylant

Illustrations by D.H. Warr

REFLECTION PUBLISHING

Published by Reflection Publishing
1 Hendrick Drive, Abilene, Texas 79602
www.reflectionpublishing.com

Pylant, Agnes D.
  Three Score and Ten…WOW! /Agnes D. Pylant.
—2nd ed.   248.8

Summary: Sound counsel for those 70–or any age–who want
to continue living with usefulness and fulfillment.

ISBN   0-9657561-3-0   LC   97-76187

Threescore & Ten... WOW!

Dedicated to

Two sets of longtime friends

Dr. and Mrs. John H. Maguire
(John and Clyde)

Mr. and Mrs. William E. Carroll
(Bill and Catherine)

CONTENTS

Chapter One

Chapter Two

Chapter Three

Chapter Four

Afterword

Chapter One

The Status Quo

Seventy! Me?

Can't be! Must be!

These friends and relatives have gathered to honor me on what they call a "momentous occasion." Nobody seems surprised. I resent their calm acceptance of an evident fact. Why don't they speak up and say things like:

"You're not really seventy!"

"Youngest seventy I ever saw!"

"You have the face and figure of a woman of fifty!"

They don't say anything . . .

    They hug me gently.
        They handle me with care.
            They help unwrap my gifts.

    This is a very special birthday! It is the first biblical one I've had:

    The years of our lives are threescore and
ten, or even by reason of strength fourscore;
yet their span is but toil and trouble; they are
soon gone, and we fly away.

Psalm 90:10, RSV

    Every now and then during the party, I open my mouth to say something appropriate and brilliant, but all that comes out is: "Wow!" I don't even know what "Wow" really means.

    Later . . .

    The party is over. Everything is still and quiet in my little house. I sit for a while recovering. My heart is warm toward the wonderful people who came in friendliness and love to celebrate my accomplishment.

As I live through the evening in retrospect, savoring each precious moment, I whisper, "Wow!" Why do I keep saying that silly word? Curiosity finally gets the best of me and I go to my dictionary and hunt it up.

> Wow: To overwhelm as with
>   delight or amazement.

Well, my "Wow" certainly doesn't mean I am overwhelmed with delight. So it must mean I am overwhelmed with amazement. Since I want to understand my exact condition on this my biblical birthday, I look up that word.

> Amazement: Mental stupefaction,
>   bewilderment, consternation.

That's it!

I am stupefied, bewildered, and filled with consternation. I don't like the sound of those words. Who wants to live in a state of "Wow"? Not me!

I think of the multitude of people who have reached threescore and ten, and the great number who have *passed* that milestone. I am concerned for those who are just around the corner from seventy and are approaching it with dread. Suddenly I am consumed with an urge to try to do something about the situation.

Believe me, these years on the far side of threescore and ten are the most difficult of our lives. No matter how brilliantly and sentimentally writers and speakers paint the "sunset time" of life, those of us actually living in it can't share their ecstasies. In fact, many of the negative emotions we experience during these years make us *ill*.

Doctors, psychologists, and psychiatrists agree that negative emotions can make us sick. They also agree that happy emotions have the opposite effect.

The conclusions of these men of science are not new. They date back several thousand years. The wise man Solomon said in his book of Proverbs: "A cheerful heart is a good medicine; but a downcast spirit dries up the bones" (Proverbs 17:22, RSV).

The "downcast spirit" that dries up the bones is often brought about by the seeming indifference and impatience of those nearest and dearest to us—our children and relatives.

Also, the general attitude of society toward the aging isn't exactly heartwarming. We sense a lack of the recognition, appreciation, and respect we once enjoyed.

The depressed feeling so often manifest in the retired group is aided and sharpened by dwindling finances. In times past we could pretty well take care of our needs and wants. But now our monthly checks will stretch just so far. Somehow it goes against the grain to ask for a hand-out, even from those closest to us.

Well, there are many other things that help dehydrate us. I don't like the sound of dried up bones. I don't care too much about being with people who have them. They are generally the grouchy, complaining, critical, self-pitying type. But I've heard that in old age we are what we have always been— only more so. If that's true, many of us have been a pain in the neck all our lives. On the other hand, those of us who were nice to have around from our youth are probably still rather nice to have around.

I am convinced that, whatever our condition, those things we want changed in our lives are *up to us*. That is a hard-sounding fact, but it is a fact and we might as well face it.

We can "kick against the pricks."

We can wham our heads against a stone wall.

We can throw a tantrum every morning before breakfast.

There will be no change unless it comes from the

inside of us.

There is a way to be happy and useful even when we are threescore and ten. I hasten to add, however, that unless we are Christians, we won't care for the plan or even believe it will work, and we won't try it!

Therefore, I dedicate this small volume to the "Wow" crowd who . . .

> Knows the Lord,
>
> Trusts in him implicitly,
>
> > and
>
> Is willing to make the effort!

Chapter Two

I Refuse to Dry Up
on the Stalk—
Why Should I?

"This old house" I occupy temporarily is beginning to sag and creak on its foundation. I am constantly mending it and propping it up.

But I, myself, am not about to deteriorate!

I am made in the image of God!

God is a Spirit—and so am I!

The spirit doesn't wrinkle, crumble, or decay. However, I *am* affected by the condition of my body. It slows me down! My spirit continues to prance and paw and strain against the bit. Why not? Hasn't God said: "Even in old age they will still produce fruit and be vital and green" (Psalm 92:14, TLB)?

We assume that he means "in the usual way," but that is not what he says. Somehow we can't serve at the same old pace. Besides, former opportunities are no longer offered to us.

Baffled, puzzled, unhappy, and sometimes bitter, we look for a junk pile to crawl up on. There we sit with hands folded in resignation.

What a sight! A child of God on a junk pile!

Elijah tried something like that one time. Remember how, in his discouragement, he found a cave and crawled into it? One day he heard the stern voice of God asking: "What are you doing here, Elijah?" (1 Kings 19:9).

A cave is no place for God's man—neither is a junk pile!

God meant it when he promised the "threescore and ten group" that we could still bear fruit. He meant it when he said:

He who began a good work in you will

carry it on to completion until the day of Christ Jesus.

Philippians 1:6

But it is a very special kind of service he offers us now—
It matches our strength and our days.
It has a unique requirement—time!
　　(Most of us have plenty of that.)
It earns the same reward as other types of service.

Read again the thirtieth chapter of First Samuel. When David went to war on his enemy, two hundred of his men were too weak and sick to go into battle. But David divided the spoils with them in the same proportion as with those who fought, saying:

As his part is that goeth down to the battle, so shall his part be that tarrieth by the stuff.

1 Samuel 30:24, KJV

"Tarry" is the key word in the new service. It means to linger; to wait. To those of us who have been active for so long, these words have a dull, uninteresting sound. We are accustomed to thinking of service as physical action—an up-and-at-'em kind of thing. "To tarry, to linger, to wait" seems to us synonymous with "to dillydally, to procrastinate, to loaf."

But we are wrong!

That word "wait" does not mean "just sittin' there." It means to be in expectation, to await orders. It provides opportunity for marvelous happenings.

First of all—to us!

We wait in the presence of the Most High, the open Bible before us bursting with amazing promises . . . we accept them.

> Wait on the Lord: be of good courage, and he shall strengthen thine heart: wait, I say, on the Lord.
>
> Psalm 27:14, KJV

In quietness and in confidence shall be your strength.

Isaiah 30:15, KJV

They that wait upon the Lord shall renew their strength; they shall mount up with wings as eagles; they shall run and not be weary; and they shall walk, and not faint.

Isaiah 40:31, KJV

And lo, our spirits lift! They soar high above the things that fretted us. We are conscious of the many blessings we had overlooked. With our hearts overflowing we cry out: "Thank you, Lord. Can you use me in some way today?"

He can!

There is the *listening ministry.*

It requires the lingering and waiting technique. Even ministers can't spend enough time listening, for they have so many things pressing upon them. Often their visits to the lonely and sick prove to be more or less "pop calls." Frequently, other well-meaning but busy people attempt this service, but they appear to be poised on the edge of the chair, ready for flight at any moment.

You and I have time to listen!

One day a lonely lady in a nursing home said to me: "When you come again, bring your crocheting and stay awhile and let's talk." What she really meant was: ". . . and let me talk to you."

You don't know people like this? They are all around you

> In your home
>> Next door
>>> Down the street
>>> In nursing homes.

You don't have to do much talking yourself. You don't have to know the answers to their problems. You just have to . . . care and listen.

There is the *praying ministry.*

All of us believe in the efficacy of prayer. There is a great deal of talking and preaching and teaching and singing about prayer. But there is not enough *praying!*

There are many excellent books on the subject. We should read them. But the ministry of prayer is praying!

Our Lord's brother declared: "The prayer of a righteous man is powerful and effective" (James 5:16).

Mary, Queen of Scots, once said: "I fear the prayers of John Knox more than an army of ten thousand men!"

Private prayer, yes, the intercessory type. Not just prayer for ourselves and our aches and pains and troubles. We must pray for:

Our folks and their problems,

Our pastor and the church,

The missionaries,

The sick,

Those of our acquaintance who do not

know God,
Our dear friends—and the
    people who do not like us,
Peace in the world,
The President of our nation and those
    who advise and serve with him,
The state officials and community
    leaders...

Oh, there is no end to the list!

Pray aloud with those you have heard in your "listening ministry." To be able to pray with people so that they are helped by the prayer has been called a *magnificent talent*. It will develop and grow in power as we use it.

I have a dear friend who retired recently. He had been a beloved pastor for many years and then an effective and valued leader in his denomination. For a while, after his retirement, invitations to preach here and there came regularly. He was interim pastor in several churches while they searched for a new minister.

Then the calls became fewer, and it seemed to him that he was gradually being edged off the scene.

But that man has a talent, a sacred gift which will make him a valuable servant of God for as long as he lives . . . he can pray! I have known only one other person who could pray me right into the throne-room of God as can this man.

> As he prays,
> I worship.
> As he talks to the great God with awe-some reverence and yet with childlike confidence,
> I find my troubles melting away.

Not long ago I was in his home when he had one of his rarin'-to-mount-the-pulpit spells. He wanted to preach! I said to him:

"You have such a marvelous ministry open to you—the praying ministry. What you do for me when you pray, you can do for others. Think of going into hospitals and nursing homes, into homes where there is sorrow and misery and sin. And after listening in that attentive, loving way you have, taking those needy ones to the Lord in prayer! Think of leaving those people with a new light in their eyes and a new hope in their hearts.

"You are a powerful preacher, but you are also a gifted pray-er."

There are other splendid facets to the tarrying ministry, but these two—the listening ministry and the praying ministry—are the most far-reaching. And they are available to all of us, even the bedridden and those who live in wheelchairs.

Who would say that the tarrying ministry is easy! Those still in harness, active day and night, dashing here and there to do this and that, have it soft in comparison!

Chapter Three

I Refuse to Worry About the Future— Why Should I?

I refuse to worry about the future, because the Bible says:

> Don't worry about anything; instead pray about everything; tell God your needs and don't forget to thank Him for His answers. If you do this you will experience God's peace, which is far more wonderful than the human mind can understand. His peace will keep your thoughts and your hearts quiet and at rest as you trust in Christ Jesus.
>
> Philippians 4:6-7, TLB

I refuse to worry about the future, for

> I know whom I have believed, and am

persuaded that he is able to keep that which
I have committed unto him against that day.

2 Timothy 1:12, KJV

I refuse to worry about the future

For I am convinced that neither death nor
life, neither angels nor demons, neither the
present nor the future, nor any powers, neither height nor depth, nor anything else in
all creation, will be able to separate us from
the love of God that is in Christ Jesus our
Lord.

Romans 8:38-39

I refuse to worry about the future, for "my God
will meet all your needs according to his glorious
riches in Christ Jesus" (Phillipians 4:19).

What more do we need than these wonderful
words of the Bible!

Still we

worry

worry
worry !

As if Jesus himself had not told us in the plainest language:

Do not worry about your life, what you shall eat or drink; or about your body, what you will wear… saying, "What shall we eat?" Or "What shall we drink?" Or "What shall we wear?"… But seek first his kingdom and his righteousness, and all these things shall be given to you as well.

Matthew 6:25,31,33

I believe Him!

I can testify that our God keeps his promises.

Sometimes I feel like the widow of Zarephath we read about in the seventeenth chapter of First Kings. This is what happened: Elijah asked her for a piece of bread to eat. He was hungry.

"As surely as the Lord your God lives,"

she replied, "I don't have any bread—only a handful of flour in a jar and a little oil in a jug. I am gathering a few sticks to take home and make a meal for myself and my son, that we may eat it—and die."

Elijah said to her, "Don't be afraid. Go home and do as you have said. But first make a small cake of bread for me from what you have and bring it to me, and then make something for yourself and your son. For this is what the Lord, the God of Israel, says: 'The jar of flour will not be used up and the jug of oil will not run dry until the day the Lord gives rain on the land.'"

She went away and did as Elijah had told her. So there was food every day for Elijah and for the woman and her family. For the jar of flour was not used up and the jug of oil did not run dry, in keeping with the word of the Lord spoken by Elijah.

1 Kings 17:12-16

For me, this is a daily experience. There is always
flour in my jar
and
oil in my jug!

I *will* confess there are times when I can see the bottom of the jar through the flour.

May God forgive me for not believing him when he makes us a promise. I read the following lines in Mrs. Charles E. Cowman's book, *Traveling Toward Sunrise*:

God makes a promise,
Faith believes it,
Hope anticipates it,
Patience quietly awaits it.

What a pity we can't take God at his word and enjoy the daily care so lovingly and adequately provided for us. Instead we *look* unhappy, *act* unhappy, *are* unhappy. Why? Perhaps because we fear that we may become helpless as we grow older and there will be no one to care for us, or that we may become a burden.

We should be striding along on his promises, singing as we go:

> 'Tis so sweet to trust in Jesus,
> And to take Him at His word;
> Just to rest upon His promise,
> And to know, 'Thus saith the Lord.'

Years ago I heard this story: It was growing dark when a man from the deep South came to a river in the far North. He had to cross that river, for his destination lay on the other side. The river was frozen over. There was no bridge. The man, having had no experience with such rivers, didn't know what to do. He wasted time trying to decide whether or not the ice would hold his weight until he was safe on the other side.

Finally, realizing he had no choice, the man decided to take the chance. Strapping his bag on his back and getting down on hands and knees, ever so cautiously he inched along, dreading every moment the sound of cracking ice, the sudden plunge into icy waters.

Abruptly he stopped dead still. In the far distance he thought he heard sounds like the pounding of horses' hooves. Nearer and nearer they came until, just a few feet ahead of him, swept a huge sleigh, drawn by two powerful horses and loaded with great logs. Hazily he caught sight of the driver, a big fat man who was singing lustily on his way.

As the sounds died away across the river, how foolish the traveler felt! How thankful the darkness hid him, and that the driver hadn't seen him! How he would have laughed at the ridiculous sight of a man weighing no more than a hundred and fifty pounds, warily creeping over a frozen ice bed capable of holding tons!

Shame on us little Christians! Standing on the promises of God, upheld by his mighty hand; yet we tremble with fear that the promises will not hold or that our God will withdraw his hand.

Has he ever?

If our faith wavers and our courage is shaky as we "round the bend" at threescore and ten, a backward look over the way we have come will strengthen us for the future that still lies ahead.

How zig-zagged the path looks!

>At one place we missed the way entirely
>We took the wrong fork at another.
>How often we have turned to the right hand
>or to the left when we should have kept
>>straight ahead.

But notice—

>We always made it back to the main highway
>>and
>>Here we are!

Let us set up our own personal altar at this place. Let us call it "Ebenezer" as Samuel did. It means: "Thus far has the Lord helped us." We can testify that he has! We have seen it with our own eyes in

that backward look. It isn't likely that he will aban-
don us at this point, so let's get going!

We haven't arrived yet. Do you remember a song
from way, way back? I think the title was "Farther
On." I haven't seen it, heard it, or even thought of it
in years.

> Farther on! Still go farther;
> Count the milestones, one by one.
> Jesus will forsake you never;
> It is better farther on.

I believe that! In fact, confidentially, the thought that
I should have to live on endlessly here and never go
to the heavenly home would be unbearable.

Let's claim a few more precious promises for the
rest of the journey and then take off! God says:

> Fear not, for I have redeemed you . . .
>> You are mine.
> When you pass through the waters,
>> I will be with you;
> And when you pass through the rivers,

They will not sweep over you . . .
For I am the Lord, your God!

Isaiah 43:1-3

Jesus says:

In my Father's house are many rooms; if
it were not so, I would have told you. I am
going there to prepare a place for you. And if
I go and prepare a place for you, I will come
back and take you to be with me that you also
may be where I am.

John 14:2-3

Now the thing that sets my heart at rest and
pleases me most in these promises is the fact that "I
won't have to cross Jordan alone."

I have always dreaded trying to find my way in
a strange city. I may know the name of the street
and the number of the house I'm seeking. But there
are so *many* streets and so *many* houses, and there
never appears to be any system to their arrangement.

Invariably I have become confused and tense and very unhappy.

But not anymore!

I have solved the problem!

I just stop at the first convenient telephone booth inside the city limits and call the daughter, or friend, or school, or club, or whoever is expecting me, and I say: "I am at such and such a place. Please come get me."

It's as easy as that. In just a little while I'm being guided expertly through the labyrinth of streets to my destination. All I have to do is *follow*.

But entering the Holy City is even better than that:

Even to your old age and gray hairs
I am he, I am he who will sustain you.
I have made you and I will carry you;
I will sustain you and I will rescue you.

Isaiah 46:4

Worry about the future? Why should I? My Lord

has made more than adequate provision for me.

Worry about the future? Not if I really believe that

> No eye has seen,
> no ear has heard,
> no mind has conceived
> what God has prepared for those that
> love him.

1 Corinthians 2:9

It is an exciting and thrilling adventure that awaits us. We have been talking and singing about Jesus for so long. . . . Now, we actually are going to be with him! In the words of David: "Such knowledge is too wonderful for me, too lofty for me to attain" (Psalm 139:6). Or, as we might say, "It is such a tremendous thought I can't take it in."

Well, we don't have to take it in. Everything is arranged. So let's leave it there and get on with the business of living now, right where we are . . .

Loving people,

Serving them within the limits of our ability, and
Trusting our Lord moment by moment, being
     happy in the knowledge that
"As far as God is concerned there is a sweet,
wholesome fragrance in our lives. It is the fragrance of Christ within us, an aroma to both
the saved and the unsaved all around us."

                              2 Corinthians 2:15, TLB

Hallelujah !

Chapter Four

I Refuse to Feel Sorry for Myself— Why Should I?

"But I am threescore and ten!" So what?

"But I am threescore and twenty!" So what?

Even if you are Mr. or Mrs. Methuselah, again I say—So what?

God doesn't seem to have put an age limit on the working power of his promises. They will stay fresh and trustworthy for as long as we live.

Read again those unbreakable promises in the preceding chapters. Read them over and over. Think about them every morning when you wake up. Rest upon them when the nighttime comes. And . . .

you
        know
               what?

A miracle will happen to you! You will lose that
      "Last rose of summer"
        "Poor me!"
          "Sniff-sniff"-look.

You will find friends beating a path to your door. Loving you. Seeking comfort and encouragement from you because *"There is just something about you!"*

Consider again that startling verse of Proverbs 17:22: "A cheerful heart is a good medicine."

This time I'm not thinking of what the cheerful-heart medicine does for you, but rather what it does for those who come near you. Being with you will be like taking an iron-fortified, vitamin-enriched tonic.

But don't forget the warning in the second half of that verse. It also applies to your friends and neighbors. Read it: "but a downcast spirit dries up the bones." Those who visit you or wait upon you or just live in the same house with you—all stand in danger of having their bones dried up!

What a gruesome thought!

What a terrible responsibility!

As we re-read this verse about the cheerful heart and its influence for good or bad, perhaps we should take a good, honest look at ourselves.

I know it isn't considered good form to approach anything from a negative viewpoint, but I think a good jolt might stun us into seeing ourselves more realistically.

Did you ever see a chicken with the pip? Its eyelids are so heavy it can hardly see. Its feathers drag the ground. It moves slowly, lifting its little feet as if each step will be the last. A sad and sorry sight is a chicken with the pip. Down where I live, we shoot 'em!

Now don't get me wrong. I'm not suggesting that

all the poor pip-looking old folks be shot. But I am suggesting that the threescore and ten crowd take Proverbs 17:22 very seriously.

The writings of Dr. Halford Luccock have always impressed me. They are so different. They make me laugh even while I'm getting the sharp point. He said that sometimes, as he sat on the platform on Sunday morning, looking out over his congregation, he got the feeling that they had all met to mourn a defeat rather than to celebrate a victory. He said it seemed to him that the congregation was moving slowly and arthritically down toward the cemetery. He became so depressed he didn't feel like preaching the sermon he had prepared.

One morning Dr. Luccock met a member of his flock on the street. "Good morning, friend," he said with a smile. "How are you this morning?" The man turned doleful eyes toward his pastor. The corners of his mouth had a decided downward droop. Without a particle of expression in face or voice he replied: "Fine, thank you. Just fine."

"Then," said Dr. Luccock in a confidential manner, "why don't you tell your face about it?"

In his book *For Our Age of Anxiety* Dr. Lofton Hudson has a chapter on Christian joy. There is a paragraph in it worth the price of the entire volume. I can't quote it exactly but this is the idea: When I consider all the glum, gloomy, negative, halfhearted Christians I know, it is no wonder the kingdom of God progresses so slowly. Many of us have that sad-sack, prison-house, God-help-us, kind of religion. There is no luster about us, no stars in our eyes, no joy bells in our hearts, no hallelujahs in our lives.

I love people with hallelujahs in their lives. I enjoy being with folks who have a luster about them.

I believe with all my heart that it is possible to keep the luster and the joy bells and the stars and the hallelujahs on and on
>past threescore and ten
>>past threescore and twenty
>>>past threescore and whatever!

And now I've come to the "in conclusion" or "finally brethren" part of this little book.

You may be wondering why I've chosen to place the chapter on self-pity last. Wouldn't one of the chapters dealing with the future be more logical?

Oh, no!

It is precisely the promises quoted in Chapters Two and Three that leave us with no excuse for feeling sorry for ourselves. The promises of Chapter Two tell us that we need not fear becoming useless to the Lord. We don't have to dry up on the stalk or to allow ourselves to be relegated to dusty shelves and junk piles. The promises of Chapter Three assure us that we have no cause to worry about the future.

Therefore, we can close on a note of triumph and praise!

I have heard several choirs composed of senior adults, and they were all good. But one stands out in my memory above them all. It was called The Amazing Grace Choir.

I am sure there wasn't a member under sixtyfive. Since the choir loft of their church would accommodate only fifty members, there was a waiting list—a long waiting list.

The night I heard them sing and testify, I broke out in goose bumps half an inch high! They used no songbooks. They sang the messages of joy and hope straight from their hearts to the audience. There was a genuine radiance about these people. I remember their opening number:

> All creatures of our God and King,
> Lift up your voice and with us sing
>> Alleluia! Alleluia!
> Thou burning sun with golden beam,
> Thou silver moon with softer gleam!
>> O praise Him!
>> O praise Him!
>> Alleluia! Alleluia! Alleluia!

And believe it or not, they closed the program with a magnificent rendition of "The Holy City."

No drying up on the stalk here,
No worrying about the future!

If anyone felt sorry for himself, he kept it well hidden that night!

Now, I can't sing. The sound comes out pretty awful when I try, so the public has never heard me. However, since I live alone, I do a great deal of quiet singing within the confines of my little house.

And I really open up and let the rafters of my car ring as I drive along the highway. I know God doesn't pay any attention to the cracks in my voice, but accepts the praise I'm trying to express and the intent of my heart as I make this joyful noise. Luckily for the passers-by, I'm air-conditioned and can keep my windows rolled up!

I would like to make a wild suggestion: How about all of you who read this book joining me in a great unseen choir—

You way out there in

California

You somewhere on the

                East Coast

You in several of the

                states in between—

           Let's Sing!

"There's within my heart a melody;

Jesus whispers sweet and low,

'Fear not, I am with thee, peace, be still,'

In all of life's ebb and flow.

Jesus, Jesus, Jesus,

Sweetest name I know,

Fills my every longing,

Keeps me singing as I go."

Afterword

The Proof of the Pudding

It would be too bad to let this little book disappear from the market. It is ageless in its wisdom. When it first came out, I was only 36 years old; yet, even at that age, it met needs in my life and inspired me. I have re-read it frequently over the years, receiving the same inspiration. I want everybody to share the joys of Mom's insights, which came through her close fellowship with God.

After passing "three score and ten," she remained *very* active, speaking at conferences and entertaining with pantomimes, readings, and stories, often with audience participation. She was one of the few people I have known with charisma. College students in assembly gave her standing ovations. Before any audience she could say ordinary things and electrify the crowds: They would laugh; they would be uplifted; they would learn. All would be very, very glad they had come.

In her eighties, she continued to travel and speak throughout the country, but she accepted many fewer engagements. Her active life was enabled and extended by the devoted friends who would drive her to her special events or programs and would look after her every need. She would sometimes have to call on a good-looking man or two (all men were good-looking to her) to lift her onto the stage, making it all part of her act so that everyone laughed. Her strength being limited, she knew she had to spend it on first things first. The first half of every day was spent in devotion—prayer at length, Bible reading, worship. It's amazing how much her scattered family counted on her prayers. Her creative thinking and writing came from the overflow of the morning, and she definitely lived what she wrote.

One of the amazing things about her was the way she never looked back. Always looking forward, she never expressed regrets as she passed from one stage of life to the next. When she finally had to leave her little log house in Palmetto, Florida, I thought she would be tearful and sad. Instead, she was happy and bubbling as we drove to her next location—a retirement home in Jacksonville. She was full of anticipation for her next mission. "Now I am beginning my retirement home ministry!" she exclaimed more than once. When at eighty-four it was time for her to move to Virginia to be with us, she didn't even pause. As part of the family packed her few belongings and brought them overland, she and I flew the distance. Living very much in the present still and loving every minute of it, she thanked the young steward for helping her. "Your mother must be proud of you," she said, beaming up at him.

Another unusual thing about her was that she never wanted anyone to suspect she was suffering from severe arthritis. At home or when eating out, when she stood up to leave, she would pause and go through a charade of searching for something on the table in order to gain time for her legs to stabilize enough for her to walk. Then she would walk off at a spry clip, smiling and nodding to people she passed.

She never dreaded old age and never thought that she herself was old. Only three or four days after arriving in Virginia she had a stroke that totally disabled her—or did it? In her lucid moments, she would say, "It's time for my wheelchair ministry!" or make comments like, "You must take care of Lola [my mother-in-law]. I love her so." Two days later, as she was loaded onto a stretcher at the hospital, she whispered, "I'm going on my Flight F-I-N-A-L." (This was a reading she had given many times.) "I will hear them sing the 'Hallelujah Chorus'!"

She was silent for most of the remaining two months of her life, and we never knew when and if she was hearing us. We celebrated her eighty-fifth birthday with a cake and read her the stacks of cards, assuming she heard. One day at the nursing home, we had her hair spruced up with a permanent, and she saw her face in the mirror. Her face, now limp from the stroke, could no longer hold her habitually vivacious expression, and it must have been a shock to her. The next day, she said, "Patty, there are some people here who are so old . . . I love them so . . . I'm one of them. Patty, I'm old."

Three days later, she died. Even that was a joyous occasion for her. She patted the hands of those gathered around her bed and then slipped away to join her husband and Jesus.

I hope you've enjoyed her happy reminiscences and insights! They are the real thing—and really never came to an end.

Her daughter Patty
September 1998